Animal Show and Tell

Sea Animals

Élisabeth de Lambilly-Bresson

GARETH**STEVENS**

PUBLISHING

A Member of the WRC Media Family of Companies

The Crab

I am a crab.
I look like a big spider
dressed in armor.
When I tiptoe sideways
across the beach, stay away
from my big claws.
I might pinch your bare toes!

The Seagull

I am a seagull.
I walk along the beach,
looking for scraps to eat.
Then, with a shriek,
I fly away
to catch fish in the sea.

The Starfish

I am a starfish.
When I rest,
I spread out my five arms
like the rays of the Sun.
When I swim, I swirl and twirl
like a deep-sea dancer.

The Shrimp

I am a shrimp.
I have many legs for walking
on the ocean floor.
But when I swim,
I quickly spin
to keep fishing nets
from catching me.

The Hermit Crab

I am a hermit crab.
My body is very soft.
To keep it safe,
I crawl into
another animal's empty shell.
I wear it wherever I go.

The Jellyfish

I am a jellyfish.
Watch me swim!
I float like a ghost in the sea.
But do not touch me,
because . . . OUCH!
I sting just like a bee.

The Sea Urchin

I am a sea urchin.
Deep underwater,
I hide between the rocks.
You might think I am a flower,
but I am covered with stingers.
Be careful
where you put your feet!

Please visit our Web site at: www.garethstevens.com
For a free color catalog describing Gareth Stevens Publishing's
list of high-quality books and multimedia programs, call
1-800-542-2595 (USA) or 1-800-387-3178 (Canada).
Gareth Stevens Publishing's fax: (414) 332-3567.

Library of Congress Cataloging-in-Publication Data

Lambilly-Bresson, Elisabeth de.
   [Au bord de la mer. English]
   Sea animals / Elisabeth de Lambilly-Bresson. — North American ed.
     p. cm. — (Animal show and tell)
   ISBN-13: 978-0-8368-8160-8 (lib. bdg.)
   1. Marine animals—Juvenile literature. I. Title.
QL122.2.L3613   2007
591.77—dc22   2006034182

This edition first published in 2007 by
Gareth Stevens Publishing
A Member of the WRC Media Family of Companies
330 West Olive Street, Suite 100
Milwaukee, WI 53212 USA

Translation: Gini Holland
Gareth Stevens editor: Gini Holland
Gareth Stevens art direction and design: Tammy West

This edition coptright © 2007 by Gareth Stevens, Inc. Original edition copyright © 2002 by
Mango Jeunesse Press. First published as Les animinis: Au bord de la mer by Mango Jeunesse Press.

Printed in the United States of America

1 2 3 4 5 6 7 8 9 10 10 09 08 07 06